PERSIAN CATS

by Jeanne Ramsdale

Photographs by Louise Brown Van der Meid

Distributed in the U.S.A. by T.F.H. Publications, Inc., 211 West Sylvania Avenue, P.O. Box 27, Neptune City, N.J. 07753; in England by T.F.H. (Gt. Britain) Ltd., 13 Nutley Lane, Reigate, Surrey; in Canada to the book store and library trade by Clarke, Irwin & Company, Clarwin House, 791 St. Clair Avenue West, Toronto 10, Ontario; in Canada to the pet trade by Rolf C. Hagen Ltd., 3225 Sartelon Street, Montreal 382, Quebec; in Southeast Asia by Y.W. Ong, 9 Lorong 36 Geylang, Singapore 14; in Australia and the south Pacific by Pet Imports Pty. Ltd., P.O. Box 149, Brookvale 2100, N.S.W., Australia. Published by T.F.H. Publications, Inc. Ltd., The British Crown Colony of Hong Kong.

ISBN 0-8766-178-9

Contents

Though all kittens are lovable, the fluffy White Persian kitten has a special appeal. In between baths, its coat can be kept beautiful with the aid of powder shampoos, or even just plain talcum powder.

Smoke male, Ch. Uwahi Nui Nui of Fair Oaks; Sire: Ch. Nuikane Rania of Spring Mountain; Dam: Spring Mountain Cinderella; Breeder: Winifred Miles; Owner: Mr. and Mrs. Paul Raine.

1. The Persian's Background

Persian cats are the aristocrats of catdom. The glamorous coat of long, silky fur, sweet "baby" face and eyes like jewels create a living picture of regal beauty.

The Persian cat of today is the result of long-ago crossings of two similar breeds of long-haired cats—the Angora and the original Persian. Modern show standards favor the large head, short, heavy body and thick coat of the Persian. The long, fine silky-textured Angora-type fur remains desirable, but the Angora's longer body and smaller head is obsolete. The Angora cat, as a breed, is extinct. Longhair, or Persian, is the correct name.

PERSIAN STANDARDS

The following standards have been adopted by the Cat Fanciers' Association Inc.

The scale of points varies slightly in some of the other national organizations, but the requirements are basically the same in all. The standard sets forth the "perfect cat," which is what we strive for in breeding. No one, yet, has achieved perfection in every detail, but the general level continues to improve toward this end. The faults and objections mentioned are tendencies to throw back to original ancestry in type and coloring. There are some characteristics originally arranged by nature, to help the cats meet challenges of survival and habitat. This, of course, is no longer a factor with domesticated cats, so the stress is entirely on eye-appeal. All of the colors are equally beautiful—the one for you is whatever you like the best. The most popular colors at the present time, on the basis of the number registered with the Cat Fanciers' Association, are silver, blue, white and black. Geographical location seems to have a great influence on the popularity of a color.

And now for the standards.

HEAD: Round and massive, with great breadth of skull. Round face with round underlying bone structure. Well set on a short, thick neck.

EARS: Small, round tipped, tilted forward, and not unduly open at the base. Set far apart, and low on the head, fitting into (without distorting) the rounded contour of the head.

EYES: Large, round and full. Set far apart and brilliant, giving a sweet expression to the face.

NOSE: Short, snub and broad. With "Break."

CHEEKS: Full.

JAWS: Broad and powerful.

CHIN: Full and well-developed.

BODY: Of cobby type, low on the legs, deep in the chest, equally massive around shoulders and rump, with a short, well-rounded middle piece. Large or medium in size. Quality the determining consideration, rather than size.

BACK: Of cobby type, low on the legs, deep in the chest, equally massive across shoulders and rump, with a short, well-rounded middle piece. Large or medium in size. Quality the determining consideration, rather than size.

LEGS: Short, thick and strong. Forelegs straight.

PAWS: Large, round and firm. Toes carried close, five in front and four behind.

The painting reproduced here portrays (right) Black Smoke male, Rm. Tr. Gr. Ch. Concordia Merango Wolfgang, bred by Mrs. John Porter; and (left) Rm. Tr. Gr. Ch. Wolfgang's Madel, owned and bred by Mrs. Harriet Wolfgang.

Chinchilla female, Quint. Gr. Ch. La Chata of Veverly-Serrano; Sire: Fanfare of Allington (Imp.); Dam: Charisse of Beverly-Serrano; Breeder; Jessie Hazlett; Owner: Mr. & Mrs. E.W. Peterson.

TAIL: Short, but in proportion to body length. Carried without a curve and at an angle lower than the back.

COAT: Long and thick, standing off from the body. Of fine texture, glossy and full of life. Long all over the body, including the shoulders. The ruff immense and continuing in a deep frill between the front legs. Ear and toe tufts long. Brush very full.

DISQUALIFY: Locket or button. Kinked or abnormal tail. Incorrect number of toes.

PERSIAN COLORS

WHITE: Pure glistening white. *Nose Leather:* Pink. *Paw Pads:* Pink. *Eye Color:* Deep blue or brilliant copper. Odd-eyed whites shall have one blue and one copper eye with equal color depth.

BLACK: Dense coal black, sound from roots to tip of fur. Free from any tinge of rust on tips, or smoke undercoat. *Nose Leather:* Black. *Paw Pads:* Black or Brown. *Eye Color:* Brilliant Copper.

BLUE: Blue, lighter shade preferred, one level tone from nose to tip of tail. Sound to the roots. A sound darker shade is more acceptable than an unsound lighter shade. *Nose Leather:* Blue. *Paw Pads:* Blue. *Eye Color:* Brilliant Copper.

RED: Deep, rich, clear, brilliant red; without shading, markings or ticking. Lips and chin the same color as coat. *Nose Leather:* Brick Red. *Paw Pads:* Brick Red. *Eye Color:* Brilliant Copper.

CREAM: One level shade of buff cream, without markings. Sound to the roots. Lighter shades preferred. *Nose Leather:* Pink. *Paw Pads:* Pink. *Eye Color:* Brilliant Copper.

CHINCHILLA: Undercoat pure white. Coat on back, flanks, head, and tail sufficiently tipped with black to give the characteristic sparkling silver appearance. Legs may be slightly shaded with tipping. Chin and ear tufts, stomach and chest, pure white. Rims of eyes, lips and nose outlined with black. *Nose Leather:* Brick Red. *Paw Pads:* Black. *Eye Color:* Green or Blue-Green.

SHADED SILVER: Undercoat white with a mantle of black tipping shading down from sides, face, and tail from dark on the ridge to white on the chin, chest, stomach, and under the tail. Legs to be the same tone as the face. The general effect to be much darker than a chinchilla. Rims of eyes, lips and nose outlined with black. *Nose Leather:* Brick Red. *Paw Pads:* Black. *Eye Color:* Green or Blue-Green.

CHINCHILLA GOLDEN: Undercoat rich warm cream. Coat on back, flanks, head and tail sufficiently tipped with seal brown to give golden appearance. Legs may be slightly shaded with tipping. Chin and ear tufts, stomach and chest, cream. Rims of eyes, lips and nose outlined with seal brown. *Nose Leather:* Deep Rose. *Paw Pads:* Seal Brown. *Eye Color:* Green or Blue-Green.

SHADED GOLDEN: Undercoat rich warm cream with a mantle of seal brown tipping shading down from sides, face, and tail from dark on the ridge to cream on the chin, chest, stomach, and under the tail. Legs to be the same tone as the face. The general effect to be much darker than a chinchilla. Rims of eyes, lips and nose outlined with seal brown. *Nose Leather:* Deep Rose. *Paw Pads:* Seal Brown. *Eye Color:* Green or Blue-Green.

SHELL CAMEO (Red Chinchilla): Undercoat white, the coat on the back, flanks, head, and tail to be sufficiently tipped with red to give the characteristic sparkling appearance. Face and legs may be very slightly shaded with tipping. Chin, ear tufts, stomach, and chest white. *Nose Leather:* Rose. *Rims of Eyes:* Rose. *Paw Pads:* Rose. *Eye Color:* Brilliant Copper.

SHADED CAMEO (Red Shaded): Undercoat white with a mantle of red tipping shading down the sides, face, and tail from dark on the ridge to white on the chin,

The coal Black Persian with its contrasting copper-colored eyes presents a striking appearance. The deeper the color of the eyes, the better. Blacks present a problem in keeping their coats truly black, but various grooming and dietary techniques can be used to help.

The Cameo-colored Persian is a recent newcomer to the acceptable colors in this breed. At first glance he appears to be cloaked in an aura of golden light. The effect is achieved by the white hairs shading to cream through copper and red at the tops.

chest, stomach, and under the tail. Legs to be the same tone as face. The general effect to be much redder than the Shell Cameo. *Nose Leather:* Rose. *Rims of Eyes:* Rose. *Paw Pads:* Rose. *Eye Color:* Brilliant Copper.

SHELL TORTOISESHELL: Undercoat white. Coat on the back, flanks, head, and tail to be delicately tipped in black with well defined patches of red and cream tipped hairs as in the pattern of the Tortoiseshell. Face and legs may be slightly shaded with tipping. Chin, ear tufts, stomach, and chest white to very slightly tipped. *Eye Color:* Brilliant Copper. Blaze of red or cream tipping on face is desirable.

SHADED TORTOISESHELL: Undercoat white. Mantle of black tipping and clearly defined patches of red and cream tipped hairs as in the pattern of the Tortoiseshell. Shading down the sides, face, and tail from dark on the ride to slightly tipped or white on the chin, stomach, legs, and under the tail. The general effect is to be much darker than the Shell Tortoiseshell. *Eye Color:* Brilliant Copper. Blaze of red or cream tipping on the face is desirable.

BLACK SMOKE: White undercoat, deeply tipped with black. Cat in repose appears black. In motion the white undercoat is clearly apparent. Points and mask black with

Silver tabby female, Gr. & Quint. Ch. Silver Vista Jade; Sire: Crusade of Pensford (Imp.); Dam: Triple Ch. Lady Lou of Katnip Korner; Owned and bred by Mrs. Elissa Elder.

narrow band of white at base of hairs next to skin which may be seen only when the fur is parted. Light silver frill and ear tufts. *Nose Leather:* Black. *Paw Pads:* Black. *Eye Color:* Brilliant Copper.

BLUE SMOKE: White undercoat, deeply tipped with blue. Cat in repose appears blue. In motion the white undercoat is clearly apparent. Points and mask blue with narrow band of white at base of hairs next to skin which may be seen only when fur is parted. White frill and ear tufts. *Nose Leather:* Blue. *Eye Color:* Brilliant Copper.

CAMEO SMOKE (Red Smoke): White undercoat, deeply tipped with red. Cat in repose appears red. In motion the white undercoat is clearly apparent. Points and mask red with narrow band of white at base of hairs next to skin which may be seen only when fur is parted. White frill and ear tufts. *Nose Leather:* Rose. *Rims of Eyes:* Rose. *Paw Pads:* Rose. *Eye Color:* Brilliant Copper.

SMOKE TORTOISESHELL: White undercoat deeply tipped with black with clearly defined, unbrindled patches of red and cream tipped hairs as in the pattern of the Tortoiseshell. Cat in repose appears Tortoiseshell. In motion, the white undercoat is clearly apparent. Face and ears Tortoiseshell pattern with narrow band of white at the base of the hairs next to the skin that may be seen only when hair is parted. White ruff and ear tufts. *Eye Color:* Brilliant Copper. Blaze of red or cream tipping on face is desirable.

CLASSIC TABBY PATTERN: Markings dense, clearly defined and broad. Legs evenly barred with bracelets coming up to meet the body markings. Tail evenly ringed.

This beautiful Persian enjoys the closeness of her kitten.

Black male, Gr. Ch. Pied Piper of Barbe Bleue; Sire: Double Ch. Barbe Bleue Personality; Dam: Barbe Bleue Mandy; Breeder: Peggy Harbaugh; Owner: Bess Morse.

Several unbroken necklaces on neck and upper chest, the more the better. Frown marks on forehead form intricate letter "M." Unbroken line runs back from outer corner of eye. Swirls on cheeks. Vertical lines over back of head extend to shoulder markings which are in the shape of a butterfly with both upper and lower wings distinctly outlined and marked with dots inside outline. Back markings consist of a vertical line down the spine from butterfly to tail with a vertical stripe paralleling it on each side, the three stripes well separated by stripes of the ground color. Large solid blotch on each side to be encircled by one or more unbroken rings. Side markings should be the same on both sides. Double vertical row of buttons on chest and stomach.

MACKEREL TABBY PATTERN: Markings dense, clearly defined, and all narrow pencillings. Legs evenly barred with narrow bracelets coming up to meet the body markings. Tail barred. Necklaces on neck and chest distinct, like so many chains..Head barred with an "M" on the forehead. Unbroken lines running back from the eyes. Lines running down the head to meet the shoulders. Spine lines run together to form a narrow saddle. Narrow pencilings run around body.

11

PATCHED TABBY PATTERN: A Patched Tabby (Torbie) is an established silver, brown, or blue tabby with patches of red and/or cream.

BROWN PATCHED TABBY: Ground color brilliant coppery brown with classic or mackerel tabby markings of dense black with patches of red and/or cream clearly defined on both body and extremities; a blaze of red and/or cream on the face is desirable. Lips and chin the same shade as the rings around the eyes. *Eye Color:* Brilliant Copper.

BLUE PATCHED TABBY: Ground color, including lips and chin, pale bluish ivory with classic or mackerel tabby markings of very deep blue affording a good contrast with ground color. Patches of cream clearly defined on both body and extremities; a blaze of cream on the face is desirable. Warm fawn overtones or patina over the whole. *Eye Color:* Brilliant Copper.

SILVER PATCHED TABBY: Ground color, including lips and chin, pale silver with classic or mackerel tabby markings of dense black with patches of red and/or cream

Present in this one litter of Persian kittens are three different color categories recognized by the breed standard: Tortoise shell, Black, and Brown tabby.

This Brown tabby Persian sports the tabby markings worn by domestic short hairs as well as their long-haired cousins. In the Brown tabby, black bars stand out against a toasty warm background though the tabby stripes occur in several other color combinations that satisfy the standard for the breed also.

clearly defined on both body and extremities. A blaze of red and/or cream on the face is desirable. *Eye Color:* Brilliant Copper or Hazel.

SILVER TABBY: Ground color, including lips and chin, pale, clear silver. Markings dense black. *Nose Leather:* Brick Red. *Paw Pads:* Black. *Eye Color:* Green or Hazel.

RED TABBY: Ground color red. Markings deep, rich red. Lips and chin red. *Nose Leather:* Brick Red. *Paw Pads:* Pink. *Eye Color:* Brilliant Copper.

BROWN TABBY: Ground Color brilliant coppery brown. Markings dense black. Lips and chin the same shade as the rings around the eyes. Back of leg black from paw to heel. *Nose Leather:* Brick Red. *Paw Pads:* Black or Brown. *Eye Color:* Brilliant Copper.

13

BLUE TABBY: Ground color, including lips and chin, pale bluish ivory. Markings a very deep blue affording a good contrast with ground color. Warm fawn overtones or patina over the whole. *Nose Leather:* Old Rose. *Paw Pads:* Rose. *Eye Color:* Brilliant Copper.

CREAM TABBY: Ground color, including lips and chin, very pale cream. Markings of buff or cream sufficiently darker than the ground color to afford good contrast, but remaining within the dilute color range. *Nose Leather:* Pink. *Paw Pads:* Pink. *Eye Color:* Brilliant Copper.

CAMEO TABBY: Ground color off-white. Markings red. *Nose Leather:* Rose. *Paw Pads:* Rose. *Eye Color:* Brilliant Copper.

TORTOISESHELL: Black with unbrindled patches of red and cream. Patches clearly defined and well broken on both body and extremities. Blaze of red or cream on face is desirable. *Eye Color:* Brilliant Copper.

CALICO: White with unbrindled patches of black and red. White predominant on underparts. *Eye Color:* Brilliant Copper. DILUTE CALICO: White with unbrindled patches of blue and cream white predominant on underparts. *Eye Color:* Brilliant Copper.

BLUE-CREAM: Blue with patches of solid cream. Patches clearly defined and well broken on both body and extremities. *Eye Color:* Brilliant Copper.

BI-COLOR: Black and white, blue and white, red and white, or cream and white. White feet, legs, undersides, chest and muzzle. Inverted "V" blaze on face desirable. White under tail and white collar allowable. *Eye Color:* Brilliant Copper.

PERSIAN VAN BI-COLOR: Black and white, red and white, blue and white, cream and white. White cat with color confined to the extremities; head, tail and legs. One or two small colored patches on body allowable.

PEKE-FACE RED AND PEKE-FACE RED TABBY: The Peke-Face cats should conform in color, markings and general type to the standards set forth for the red and red tabby Persian cat. The head should resemble as much as possible that of the Pekinese dog from which it gets its name. Nose should be very short and depressed, or indented between the eyes. There should be a decidedly wrinkled muzzle. Eyes round, large, and full, set wide apart, prominent and brilliant.

POINT SCORE

Head (including size and shape of eyes, ear shape and set)...................... 30
Type (including shape, size, bone and length of tail)......................... 20
Coat... 10
Balance... 5
Refinement.. 5
Color.. 20
Eye Color.. 10

In all tabby varieties, the 20 points for color are to be divided 10 for markings and 10 for color.

14

2. Selecting Your Persian Kitten

WHERE TO BUY YOUR PERSIAN

Most Persian kittens that are for sale, either through pet shops or ads, are the products of some cattery. This is a great advantage to the buyer. Nature being what it is, some very unsuitable matches would occur unless breeding was planned. When you purchase a pedigree kitten, whether you buy the papers or not, you have the assurance that a good deal of thought and work have gone into making your kitten what he is. Personality traits, good health, and beauty of form and coat are not accidental. Your cat's pedigree is the record of how all these things have been blended for four or more generations.

If you are considering the possibility of breeding and/or showing a Persian, acquaint yourself with the standard and, if possible, attend a cat show before making your purchase. Then go to a breeder of experience and *good reputation*, and rely on his judgment of what is in your best interest.

The difference between the pet and show types is often apparent only to the trained eye. No breeder of consequence wants cats from his cattery to be shown unless they are potential winners. Show kittens or cats will of course cost a little more. They are well worth the extra initial investment if you plan to breed or show them.

A HEALTHY KITTEN

Be sure the kitten you choose is alert, with bright and clear eyes. He should be well fleshed, with a substantial feel. These are characteristics of the healthy Persian. Steer clear of a kitten with a runny nose, sore ears, skin lesions, or drab-looking, harsh-feeling coat. It is a wise precaution to have the kitten you choose checked by a veterinarian for less obvious conditions.

Cream male, Qd. Ch. Lee's Hi-Hat Champaign; Sire: Candy Kid; Dam: Ch. Kansas City Moonglo of Eden; Breeder: Mrs. George Lee; Owner: Mrs. Marie Wilson.

Special attention
to grooming must
be given this
Cream kitten and
her matching
companion.
Because of the
light color, their
coats can become
soiled easily and
both the Cocker
and kitten have
long hair that will
mat and tangle
unless brushed
regularly.

A Persian kitten should be at least 9 to 10 weeks of age before he is taken to his new home. The extra weeks with his mother, after weaning, provide a much better start in life. The kitten has also had time to get his two feline enteritis vaccinations at 8 and 9 weeks, and to build up his immunity to this common, dangerous and nearly always fatal disease. His digestive processes have developed sufficiently by this age so that a change in environment, food and water will not make him sick. More of the individual personality pattern is present, and his mother has had time to teach him the ways of life.

WHY NOT TWO KITTENS?

One kitten is fun—two kittens are more fun. Often a family finds that one kitten does not "go around" so they return to purchase another. An only cat very often gets spoiled. When you have two, they have cat companionship and competition, and they develop playing routines that defy description! If the kittens are of different sexes, you might find it more difficult if they are not spayed or neutered. It is not wise to bring up a brother and sister together unless you prevent them from interbreeding.

Kittens are mischievous—but fun!

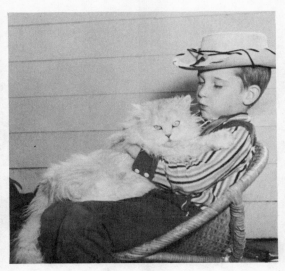

Even "Cowboys" love Persians!

MALE OR FEMALE?

Although males and females make equally good pets, each sex has different personality characteristics, just as people do. Each cat has its own individual disposition. Try to choose one that fits you. The males are usually larger and more boisterous. The females are usually more delicately built and girlish in their behaviour. Both are equally lovable in their own special ways. Unaltered females are potential mothers whether you wish it or not. Altering a male is less expensive and not a serious operation, nor does it cause him to grow fat and lazy, as is so often claimed.

An altered cat of either sex makes a better pet than one subject to the periodic urges of nature. Cats are rather intense about their love life and seem to suffer emotionally if prevented from pursuing it. When they are altered, all of this energy is diverted in other directions. They become more relaxed, playful and loving. The recommended age for altering a male is after 7 or 8 months. This is before any serious hormone activity gets started, and allows his urinary system to become more developed against possible cystitis tendencies. A female cat can come in season and become pregnant at any time after 5 months of age, although the first season usually is at about 7 to 8 months. Spaying should be done early if there is any possibility of her getting together with any male. Altered cats may be entered in cat shows to compete only against others of the same status.

After you have chosen your kitten, or he has chosen you, be prepared to enjoy his development from babyhood through adolescence, to full flower as an adult. Females generally mature to their full beauty at about 2 to 3 years. Males of 4 or 5 years of age are at their peak. The older they become, the more personality, intelligence and beauty they possess so that your ownership is a continuing pleasure.

One of the color problems breeders of the black Persian struggle against is apparent in this pair of blacks. The shadings of rust and sprinkling of white hairs are color features that must be bred out, but even with these flaws, the pair makes a charming portrait.

Often different color classifications of Persian will occur in the same litter, but here brothers and sisters closely resemble each other in their brown tabby markings.

3. Caring for Your Persian

Cattery cats usually are kept in outside houses, or cages, as well as in the home. Mine live in or out according to the circumstances.

There are many satisfactory types of construction for an outdoor house, as long as the basic requirements of comfort and protection are met. Screen wire should be placed over heavier, wide-mesh, hardware-cloth-type wire backing. Cats' claws can easily rip screen alone. Rough wire, such as chicken netting, is not desirable because it catches fur. Sufficient protection from drafts, rain, heat and cold is provided by a roof supported by at least three solid sides or flexible walls constructed so they can be closed.

The double walk-in house on page 41 has two doors, one glass-paned and the other screened. The outer screened side is open but can have a sheet of plastic

A pan such as this, with the proper absorbent litter is a must for housebreaking your kitten.

cloth inserted between the screen and frame during inclement weather. The solid back has a ventilating area near the roof, and is provided with a shelf. The cats can look out of three sides. The corrugated aluminium roof is insulated. A soaker hose can be run on the roof to cool the atmosphere on very hot days. The floor is linoleum over plywood for easy cleaning. The entire house is set up on concrete blocks for dryness and air circulation. Sleeping boxes, or beds, are provided by shelves at various levels and of course a sand pan and water bowl are musts.

The other type pictured is a four-cage up-and-down arrangement with a trap door between "floors." The top cage has a shelf on the back wall. This permits the cats a good deal of exercise in a small area, with three levels to jump to. The wire side panels between each set of two cages are removable so that various accommodations can be arranged for the tenants. Other features are similar to the walk-in house. Waterproof tarp rolls down, covering as much of the front as desired. Supplies and medicines are kept on the shelves of the wheeled cart, and food is served from the top of it.

A house trailer makes an excellent home for several cats. Outside runs can be connected to the house or cages, or there can be a separate enclosure for the cats to take turns in.

Good arrangements for your house cat to enjoy sun and air can be similarly constructed with the entrance through a window or door of your home.

GRIT BOX

A grit box, a fairly deep pan half filled with sand, dirt, shredded paper or commercial litter, is essential for your kitten. I have found the litter to be the most satisfactory, and the deodorizing and superabsorbent qualities well justify the cost. A few pieces of folded newspaper in the bottom of the pan can increase absorption and make disposal easier. I recommend putting the pan in a carton with high sides or on an island of newspapers because cats often make a great project of "covering up," and fling the grit out of the pan for some distance. If

A cat and dog can happily share the same household.

the box is too high for the baby to jump into, cut an entry in one side. If you have a very large home, it would be well to have a second bathroom set up for your pet. A very young kitten might not be able to reach one spot in time, since he will put off the necessary trip until the last minute, and if he has another nearer place to go to, it will come in handy. Kittens are nearly always good about using the pan, and only fail when ill, frightened or confused about its location. If your baby is trained to one material and you wish to change to a different type, do it gradually. Put a little of the new material with the old, gradually increasing the amount each day until the old type is entirely eliminated. We changed one cat from sand to toilet paper when we had a disposal problem in an apartment.

After each meal, place him in his grit box, and he will be housetrained very

This kitten is learning to eat "solid food."

One of the most popular Persian colors is the Blue. His soft blue-gray hue makes this color type distinctive.

Opposite:
The white Persian is the only color variety in which an odd-eye color may occur. When it does the eye colors should be a combination of the other two eye colors allowed in whites—blue and copper. The more intense the color, the more preferable it is.

quickly. You can dispose of the used grit and there will be no unpleasant cat odor about the house.

OTHER PETS IN THE HOUSEHOLD

Most Persians get along with and like, or at least tolerate, most dogs or other pets. It is best to introduce strangers to one another gradually by sight and smell and always be with them at first. By the time the new pet has acquired a familiar "house smell," you can leave him alone with another animal if no violent hostility has manifested itself. There may be a good deal of jealousy at first. You can help this situation by giving extra attention and reassurance to the jealous one. He will blame you more than the interloper for the change in his household.

DIET

If possible, feed your newly acquired cat or kitten what he has been used to eating. Change his diet gradually to avoid digestive upsets. Quite often a cat in new surroundings is not too interested in food. Exploration comes first! Do not be alarmed if this is the case. Try later with fresh food—a healthy animal will soon be hungry.

A young kitten should be fed 4 times a day, or leave fresh food for him all the time. Babies eat a little, play and sleep, and then eat a little more. Kittens from 4 to 8 months old can be fed on a more regular, 3 meals-a-day basis. A kitten's growth pattern is variable, so adjust the amount of food to his appetite. The adult cat needs only morning and evening feedings. Naturally a pregnant female or

Silver Tabby Female, Gr. Ch. Mi-Choice's Pa-Tudie of Silver Circle; Owned by Dr. and Mrs. A.H. Erickson.

nursing mother requires more food and extra calcium intake.

Individual requirements and tastes govern the amount of food served at any one time and the frequency of meals. Cats will not overeat, except, occasionally, special delicacies such as chicken, turkey, shrimp or fresh raw liver. They will usually eat more in the evening, some eating from time to time during the entire night.

Pet cats have a reputation for being fussy eaters. They will relish a certain type or brand of food one day and refuse it the next. On the other hand, some cats want only fish, liver, kidney or whatever happens to be their particular fancy.

At first, your Persian will play with his new collar and leash, but gradually he will become accustomed to it and learn what it is for.

Fortunately, in the last few years so many different kinds of foods have become available that any cat's taste should be satisfied while he is well nourished.

A varied, well-balanced diet is very important for health and beauty. A proper cat diet requires a high proportion of protein, fats and fatty acids. A cat also needs more vitamin B, B-12, and B-complex than any other animal. To see that your cat is provided with these and all the other necessary elements, keep in mind what a cat would eat if he were unconfined. In the wild state, fish, birds and other vegetable- and grain-eaters such as rabbits and mice are eaten nearly whole. It follows that meat with fat, organs, cereal, bone meal, vegetables, dairy products, fish and eggs all have a place in your cat's feeding. Some cats have loose bowels from drinking milk; other dairy products can be substituted. Raw

Cat personalities differ from individual to individual. In Persians, distinct personality types often accompany certain colors. This red and white Bi-color will make a most expressive and spirited companion.

These red and cream Persian kittens seem to have just about satisfied their curiosity over a hanging planter when something else caught their eye.

liver in quantity also can have an effect on the bowels but since it is such a valuable vitamin source, try to include some amount of it from time to time mixed with the regular food. Access to some green gowth also is desirable, for it is used as an emetic as well as a mineral source.

This is one of many types of carrying cages that are available.

Meat should be cut into bite-size pieces which will require chewing. The dry, chunk or kibbled foods are nutritious, good for jaw development and for prevention of tartar formation on the teeth.

Do not give your cat bones that will splinter when chewed.

Vitamin supplements will eliminate any possibility of deficiency in the diet. They also give added support through the different stages of growth. There are liquid products with droppers (plastic is best in case they are accidentally bitten), or powdered forms to sprinkle on food.

Fresh water should be available to your kitten or cat at all times. Cats often drink water out of flower vases; water seems extra tasty this way. Many cats enjoy playing in or with water.

TRAINING

Kittens and cats are easily toilet-trained; however, training them to do or not to do other things is more difficult. A very good way of training a cat to come to you whenever you want him to is always to whistle for him when it is mealtime. Rather shrill notes seem to get the best action and are readily heard, even outdoors. Your cat will also learn his name if addressed with it rather than being called "kitty". If he learns to answer only to his name, it will provide a safeguard against his being lured away by a stranger.

A cat seems to be impressed by noise and commotion. Sharp clapping of hands and loud noises with a paper will at least make him pause in the course of wrongdoing. Try to make it appear as if the interesting, forbidden object—such as the bird, furniture, rug or door—is itself attacking him with noise. Your cat will learn the meaning of "No!" even if he doesn't always wish to admit it. He will respond to praise and love and, in general, will want to please you. You'll

Begin combing
and brushing your
cat while he is
very young, so
that he may
become
accustomed to
daily grooming.

soon realize that your pet is like a small child—he will do anything to get your attention, even actions he knows will be frowned upon. He will also misbehave to express his displeasure at your actions—such as leaving him alone!

If you set up a scratching post, you will take your cat's mind and claws off the furniture and rugs. Kittens often pretend scratching posts are real trees, and do some fancy tricks on them. Nail clippers made specially for use on cats or dogs can be used to good advantage, particularly to curb the tendency of a young kitten to climb hand over hand on everything.

HARNESS AND LEASH

A Persian cat can be trained to a harness and leash. A collar is not recommended because it can rub the fur off the ruff and cause matting and bare spots beneath. It's also easy for the cat to pull his head out of a collar. The best harness is a figure 8 style, pictured elsewhere   This is easily put on and fastens on top so hair doesn't get caught in the buckle. It will be almost impossible for your pet to choke on or pull out of this type. One loop goes in an oval around his head and shoulders and the other goes under the belly to the back. With a soft leather harness there is little friction on the fur.

A young cat will consider a leash just something to play with. At first he will often act as though he can't walk or stand up with a harness on. This phase passes with practice. The harness and leash can be attached outside if your yard is protected from visiting cats, dogs and children who would have the advantage

This wide-eyed Calico kitten is pondering the passage of time—or is he hatching a kittenish plot for breaking into the hour glass and playing in the sand?

in fights with your pet. Be careful to tie the leash where it cannot get wound around anything.

If he is allowed to run loose outdoors, you can buy an elastic cat collar that will allow him to pull his head free if the collar gets caught on a fence. You might want to protect the birds by having your cat wear a bell, but remember that the bell will warn mice as well. If your Persian wanders far from home, an identification tag for his collar is a wise investment.

GETTING AROUND WITH YOUR CAT

Whenever you take your Persian out of the house or yard, he should be in a carrier or on a leash. There are several reasons why this is desirable and important. Since he is not used to the outside world, sudden noises or movements can startle and frighten him, resulting in his escape or your getting scratched or bitten. Riding in the car is easier for both of you. If he is in a transparent carrier or one with a window, you can set him up high enough to see out if he wants to. He does not get bounced around and you do not have to watch out for him underfoot, or when windows and doors are opened. You can cover the carrier wholly or partially if you have to leave him alone in the car so that "catnappers" won't be tempted. Also, on a trip to the veterinarian, your cat is not exposed to other cats' diseases or curious strange dogs. The carrier, if left open in the house, becomes a familiar place of refuge when he is exposed to unsettling experiences.

The cat carrier for Persians should be well-ventilated with room inside for toilet conveniences. If it has a wire top, a cloth or plastic cover can protect him from the sun or weather. The carrier pictured elsewhere is very satisfactory for all traveling purposes and can also double as a drying cage when turned on its side.

GROOMING

Even when your kitten is so young that combing is not strictly needed, it is good to have a daily stint with the brush and comb. This gets you and the kitten into the grooming habit. The comb should be made of steel, with long, slim teeth to get all the way through the fur to the skin. Use a comb with wide-set teeth first to straighten out the tangles and break up large accumulations of knotted fur. Then switch to a finer toothed comb to pick up loose fur and get out the small knots which can otherwise build up to matted spots. Get a very fine-toothed comb for removing fleas, and also to use on the shorter face fur. Some combs are available with two sizes of teeth.

Pay particular attention to the flanks, the back of hind legs or "pants", insides of both front and hind legs, tummy, under the chin and chest and behind the ears. These are the potential trouble spots, especially when the undercoat is shedding out. Some people unknowingly just comb the back, head and tail and find, to their sorrow, that the underside has become felted into a solid mattress of fur. This condition requires the scissors or a trip to the veterinarian.

After combing, brush against the grain of the fur to stimulate growth and to improve gloss. Fur around the neck or "ruff" should be combed and brushed up

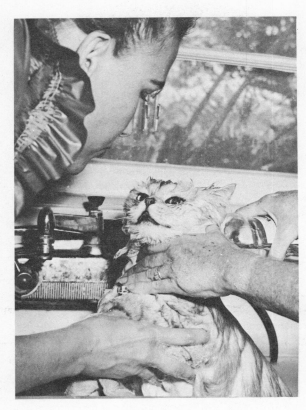

Your cat may be afraid during the first bath. Be sure to have an assistant.

and out to form an Elizabethan collar, or frame, for the face. A natural-bristle brush causes less static electricity and hair breakage than a brush made of nylon bristles.

If your cat's ears are oily, clean them gently with a cotton swab as often as necessary.

Regular grooming of a long-haired cat is very important. There will be fewer hairs around the house and even when shedding your cat will maintain his health and beauty, with fewer hairballs to be ingested and less chance of sore skin due to knots and matting.

BATHING YOUR PERSIAN CAT

If you comb and brush your Persian every day there will be little need to bathe him. I have found the powder shampoos and cleaners very helpful for spot cleaning. Cornstarch or talcum powder also can be used. In places where it is difficult for a cat to wash himself—behind and in front of the ears, under the chin, and down the bib—the fur is apt to get a little oily or greasy. Part the fur

Indoor cats should be taught that claw sharpening must take place only on a scratching post, and not on the living room furniture. Some scratching posts come equipped with catnip to help attract the cats to it.

4. Protecting the Health of Your Persian

When a kitten or cat shows little interest in food, or has diarrhea for more than a day, he needs attention. Cats generally are very healthy so if they are "off" for any length of time, there is some reason for it. Not eating and/or loose bowels is symptomatic of nearly all cat ailments. Although sometimes the reason is simple, prompt treatment is important. Amateur diagnosis can be harmful, expensive and may cost your cat's life. If he does not respond quickly to the suggested remedies for minor ailments, consult your veterinarian immediately. In good faith and ignorance, you can do more harm by treating him yourself because so many illnesses are closely related, or have similar symptoms. The cheapest life insurance for your pet is availing yourself of your doctor's experienced skill *promptly* if anything seems abnormal.

Many of the following ailments can be avoided by keeping your cat inside where you can observe his actions and eliminate exposure to contagion.

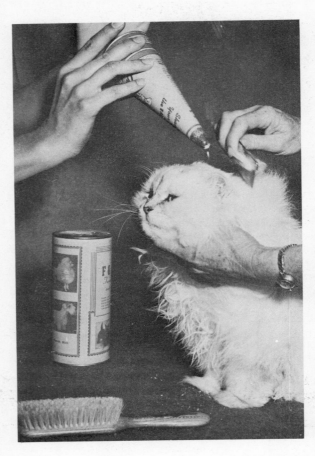

When treating your cat for fleas, use a flea powder designed especially for cats. Manufacturers of these powders have taken into account that cats groom themselves much more than dogs, ingesting a great deal of the powder, and have made the product to be non-toxic for your cat.

MAJOR DISEASES OF THE CAT

Fleas: Fleas are a common problem and are very detrimental to a Persian's health and beauty. Scratching the itching flea bites ruins the coat and causes matting, and fleas are an intermediate host to the tapeworm. Getting rid of tapeworms after you have eradicated the fleas is a job for the veterinarian.

Evidence of fleas are grains of "flea dirt" on the cat's skin and throughout the coat. This is a black substance, gritty to the touch, which turns red when wet.

With persistent effort you can completely eliminate fleas on your house cat. Your cat is not exposed to reinfestation if he is kept inside. However, flea eggs drop off the cat, the larvae hatch in various places around the house, then enter a pupa stage and later emerge as adult fleas and jump back aboard the cat. Wash all washable articles and vacuum often, particularly in the dark corners and crevices. Sprinkle flea powder on and under rugs and furniture cushions.

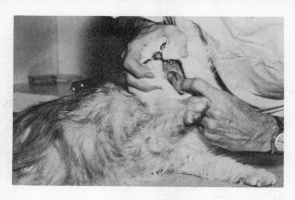

Check your cat's teeth periodically to be sure that they are free from tartar accumulation.

Be sure you use a preparation made especially for *cats*. New flea-killing preparations that are very effective and nontoxic to cats contain 4 to 5 per cent Malathion as the active ingredient. A small amount on the back of the neck and the base of the tail, applied daily for 10 days to two weeks, should rid your cat of fleas. Follow up with biweekly applications and cleaning until you are sure there are no more.

Other flea-control products work on the principle of dehydrating the insect. These claim long-lasting effectiveness, particularly in furniture and sleeping places.

Hairballs: Persian cats swallow the loose hair that comes off when they clean themselves. The more thorough your cat's combing and brushing, the fewer hairs there are to accumulate in the digestive tract. These hairs ball up and form a cigar-shaped wad. Many cats will vomit these, or pass them in the bowel movement. If they do, there is no problem. Give an adult cat a weekly dosage of a teaspoonful of salad oil, white *noncarbolated* petroleum jelly, or any of the malt-flavored petrolatum products made for this purpose, to facilitate passage. A kitten should have a smaller dose. Mineral oil is *not* recommended because it may get down into the lungs and cause mechanical pneumonia. If the hairballs do not pass and cause an obstruction, it is necessary to remove them with an enema or, in extreme cases, by surgical intervention.

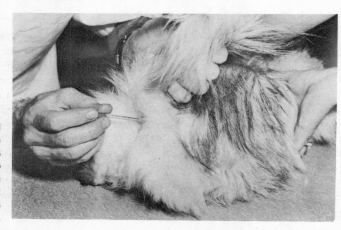

Use a rectal thermometer in this manner. It is usually best to have help in holding the cat during this procedure.

This "four cage," up and down arrangement is good, too, providing you live in an area that does not have very cold weather.

Tortoiseshell female, Ch. Kohinoor Kathleen of Moonfleet; Sire: Ch. Southlands Em Cee; Dam: Spero's Burma of Kohinoor; Breeder: Mary Kate Carrol; Owner: Mrs. E.A. Rogers.

This is an ideal double walk-in house for your cats.

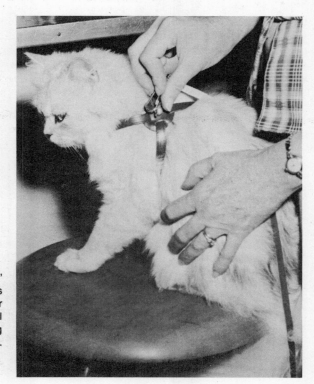

This "figure 8" type harness is the best for your Persian, for it will not cause matting and bare spots.

Diarrhea: Simple digestive upsets evidenced by loose bowels and vomiting can be treated with remedies used for children, such as Kaopectate. Two to 4 teaspoonfuls, depending on the size of the cat, given every 2 to 4 hours, should relieve these symptoms. If they persist, see the doctor.

Constipation: Difficult or infrequent bowel movements suggest the need for adjustment in the diet to produce a slightly more laxative effect. No bowel movement, especially when there is vomiting, indicates an obstruction of some nature, such as hairballs. A swallowed foreign object can also cause diarrhea or vomiting.

Fever: The normal temperature of a cat is 101 to 102°, taken rectally. Without a thermometer, you can detect fever by holding your hand across the ears and face. Pawpads also will feel burning to the touch. Excitement can cause fever. Usually, however, fever indicates an infection of some kind and as such, requires treatment of its source by the veterinarian. Occasionally, when a kitten is cutting his permanent teeth at from 3 to 7 months of age, he will run a high temperature as well as not eat because of his sore gums.

Parasites, Tapeworms, Roundworms and Ear Mites: General poor condition, lack of coat, light weight even though the appetite is good, chronic loose bowels and, in some cases, an allergic eczema reaction, can each—or all—be symptoms of parasitic infection.

Tapeworm segments, similar in appearance to grains of rice, are eliminated in the stool and can be detected there, or they stick to the fur around the anus. Deworming should be done by the veterinarian. If the powerful medicine necessary to kill the tapeworm does not pass through the cat's system in a very short time, it has to be removed by an enema; otherwise, it will poison the animal. Repeated treatment often is necessary to clear up severe cases of infestation.

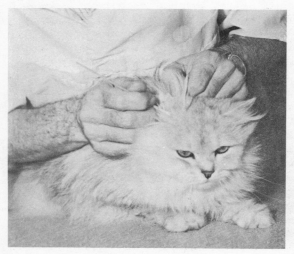

If you are in doubt about any skin irritation, take your cat to the veterinarian for diagnosis.

Hold the cat's head in this manner when administering eye medication.

The presence of roundworms can be found in a fecal analysis by the doctor. The method of treatment is the same as for tapeworms, but the medicine used is different. Roundworms are acquired from other infested animals.

Ear mites themselves are not apparent to the naked eye. The irritation of the ear canal, caused by their presence, produces a brown or black crumbly wax in and about the ears. Scratching the ears and shaking the head indicates the possibility of infestation. Ear mites are extremely contagious from and to other cats and animals. Persistent treatment with an effective product can easily clear up the condition once it is discovered.

Poisoning: Many chemicals are poisonous to cats. Particularly dangerous are DDT, Chlorodane, and Lindane in any form, as well as arsenic and coal tar derivatives such as preparations containing carbolic acid.

If you suspect poisoning, emergency treatment is to induce vomiting with repeated tablespoon doses of 3 per cent hydrogen peroxide, diluted with half water. *Then to the veterinarian immediately.* Try to identify the poison, bringing its container if possible. This will facilitate treatment since the antidote can be more quickly determined.

Skin Troubles: Some cats' skins break out due to allergies. Because ringworm and other fungus diseases can also cause this, it is vital that an expert diagnosis be made so that proper treatment can be undertaken at the doctor's direction as soon as possible. New methods, using drugs that work internally, have shown great promise for speedily eradicating ringworm. Ringworm is the only common skin disease that can be transmitted back and forth between cats and humans. Treatment is a very lengthy problem on a long-haired cat if the condition does not receive *immediate* attention.

Swellings: Swelling on any part of the body indicates injury and/or infection. A cat's skin heals very readily. Thus, a scratch or bite wound will seal over on top, outwardly showing no break, but infection can be running rampant beneath and throughout the system. Treatment, after lancing and antibiotic injections, consists mainly of keeping the scab removed so the wound can heal from the inside out.

A spray attachment such as this is most helpful when bathing your cat.

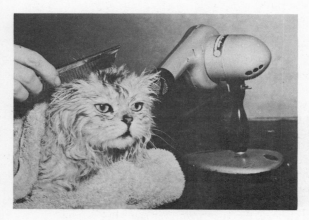

It is most important that you dry your cat thoroughly after a bath. If you have a hair dryer, by all means use it.

Blue Cream Female, Gr. and Qd. Ch. Rocky Mt. Mariposa of Vernamac; Sire: Tr. Ch. Rocky Mt. Butterscotch; Dam: Imp. Ch. Camber Sally of Rocky Mt.; Breeder Mrs. Sammy Hirsig; Owner: Mr. Nat. McKelvey.

Transparent carrying cases like this one are advantageous because your pet is often calmed by being able to see its surroundings when it is taken out of a familiar environment.

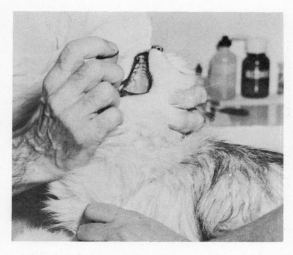

When administering a pill or capsule, push it down quickly with your index finger, and then rub the cat's throat.

Teeth: Teeth should be checked for tartar accumulations. When tartar is present, the teeth should be scaled to prevent irritation of the gums and opportunity for infection. Infected teeth should be removed.

Cystitis: Blockage of the passage of urine can cause uremic poisoning and a swift death. This can be caused by a mucous plug forming in the urethra due to the irritation of a bladder infection. It can also result from "sand" originating in the bladder, packing together, and becoming too large to pass. Stoppage is more common in the male cat because the channel is smaller. If your cat goes to the pan frequently and strains, eliminating only a small amount of urine painfully, see about it immediately. This symptom of straining during urination is commonly mistaken as being due to constipation.

Virus Diseases and Vaccinations: Although any warm-blooded animal can contract rabies, cats are not usually vaccinated against it unless there is an epidemic in the area. It is required for certain interstate or foreign travel. There are many types of viruses and germs which can cause any number of diseases, but these are more or less rare occurrences in cats. The following are exceptions.

Feline Distemper (also known as *Cat Fever* or *Feline Enteritis*): This is a specific disease of cats which has no connection with dog distemper or non-specific enteritis—a term used to describe any inflammation of the cat's intestinal tract. Kittens can, and should, be vaccinated against this deadly disease at an early age—8 to 9 weeks or as soon thereafter as possible. Young cats are particularly susceptible, although a cat of any age can contract it. Booster shots can be given as a further precaution every year or two, or more often if there is an outbreak in your neighborhood. Onset of the disease is characterized by weakness, vomiting of a yellowish fluid, diarrhea of the same type of fluid, fever and hanging of the head over a water dish. If an unvaccinated cat shows these symtoms, rush him to the veterinarian for serum treatment. The course to death is often so swift that the disease is mistaken for poisoning.

When trimming your cat's nails, be extremely careful not to clip too close, for there is a vein that runs through the nail that must not be severed.

Pneumonitis and Other Respiratory Infections: The symptoms of these diseases resemble a human's severe cold. The eyes water, the nose runs, the throat is sore, the sufferer coughs and sneezes and seems to be sore all over to the touch. He is feverish, listless and will not eat. Sometimes the bowels are loose. Treatment in the early stages gives the best and quickest results. There have been several viruses isolated which cause similar symptoms. Vaccinations have been developed against some of the more common ones and are a good precaution to take. Immunity, however, is not long-lasting and vaccination has to be repeated periodically. A cat who has recovered can have recurrences, or can be a carrier without symptoms himself, infecting other cats with whom he comes in contact.

Red female, Ch. Shawnee's Copper Lustre; Sire: Spoon River Cardinal of Shawnee; Dam: Shawnee Apache Topaz; Owned and bred by Mrs. Nikki Horner.

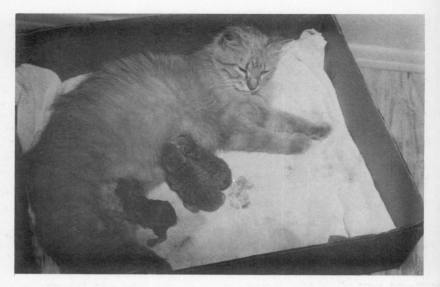

Maintain the mother and kittens in a box such as this, with some soft cloth at the bottom, then the mother can leave the kittens for a while, but the kittens cannot climb out.

5. Breeding Your Persian and Raising Kittens

Breeding Persian kittens is a specialized field. Do not undertake it without careful consideration of what would be involved in time, effort and adequate facilities for the care and sale of the prospective family. If you do want to have a litter of kittens, maintain close contact with an experienced breeder and your veterinarian through all of the phases to prevent costly errors.

WHEN TO BREED

Your breeder can help you select the best mate for your female and give you valuable advice about family traits. The mating should be planned and arranged for in advance of the actual breeding time. The female cat comes in season, or "heat," during the late winter and early spring months. She continues to "come in" on an average of once every 4 weeks, or oftener, for a period of 3 to 7 days each time until she is bred. Frequency and duration vary considerably. The female can conceive at any time during the period. She will continue to accept a male during the entire interval, which can result in mixed parentage if she is allowed outdoors after service from the wanted stud.

Blue smoke female, left, Hm. Gr. Ch. Miss Tiny's Josey-By-Joe; Blue smoke male, right, Miss Tiny's Smo-Ke-Joe; both by same parents; Sire: Qd. Ch. Marleon's Joe's Boy; Dam: Tr. Ch. Marleon Princess Aries; Owned and bred by Eileen M. Gleeson and Mary Appleman.

It is well to bring her to the male at the first sign of real "calling" or rolling. The trip and strange surroundings will often put love-making out of her mind on arrival. This is particularly true in the case of a pet cat, but after a day or so of settling down, the urge will reassert itself, and she will be agreeable to mating.

THE EXPECTANT MOTHER

The kittens are carried about 9 weeks. If you have the mother examined by a veterinarian about 3 to 4 weeks after breeding, he can usually determine how many kittens she is carrying. This is valuable information at the time of delivery. Litters usually are small, varying from one to 4 babies. The doctor will also advise you of any diet change or supplements that might be needed.

Closets are highly favored spots for having kittens. In advance of the event prepare a large cardboard box or bed with newspaper in the bottom. Provide some soft material for the mother to knead and arrange it on top of the paper. A pet cat will usually insist on you, or someone, being with her constantly before and during the delivery process.

If the mother is in hard labor for several hours without results, she may need assistance. Do not delay asking for expert help from the veterinarian; prompt care can save lives. Delivery is often difficult for Persian cats, because kittens can be large-boned and too big for her to give birth without assistance.

Black Smoke female, Gr. and Quad. Ch. Skyway's Smokey Ella, owned by Mr. and Mrs. R.M. Dalrymple. This litter, sired by Quad. Ch. Kerry Lu Smoke Gen, was unusual in that four of the kittens completed their Double Championships during their first year of showing.

An inexperienced mother sometimes does not realize the necessity of removing the covering film from the kitten's mouth and nose after birth so he can breathe. Do this yourself, immediately, if she doesn't. Severing the cord from the placenta is of less urgency.

CARING FOR THE MOTHER AND KITTENS

Once the kittens have arrived and are breathing properly and getting nourishment from their mother, there are few problems. Kittens are born blind. The eyes open at a week to 10 days of age. Keep the kittens in a dark place until their eyesight is fully developed, then gradually expose them to an increasing amount of light. If the eyelids stick back together after opening bathe the eyes with cotton soaked in a mild boric acid solution (1 teaspoon to 8 ounces of water), or just warm water. If the condition persists use an eye ointment procured from your veterinarian.

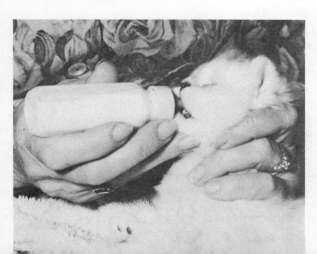

If the kittens are not getting enough nourishment, hand feed their formula with a doll's bottle in this manner.

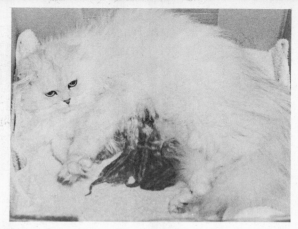

This light solid colored Persian mother gave birth to a litter of darker colored kittens, which, unlike their mother, have well delineated markings.

Check the kittens often during the first few days to see that they are being fed. They should feel fully packed and rounded within 24 hours after birth. If you have to hand feed them, use a temporary formula of half unsweetened, condensed milk and water in an eye dropper or doll bottle. Add a small amount of sugar syrup if the hand feeding persists for any length of time. Frequency of feeding depends on age and intake, on the basis of 2- to 4- hour intervals.

Ordinarily the mother will care for all the kittens' needs until they are old enough, at about 4 weeks, to climb out of the box. From this time on they gradually start to eat, lap milk and go to the sandbox at their mother's direction, with little assistance from you. Weaning usually is complete by 6 to 8 weeks of age. The mother can come in season again any time shortly after having kittens, so guard against accidental breeding. Only one litter a year is advised, unless in certain cases the female can become more run-down by constant calling than by having another family. The drain on the mother cat's system is heaviest when she is nursing, and she should be watched for signs of calcium deficiency, or eclampsia, particularly around the time the kittens are 3 to 4 weeks old, and if the litter is large.

Persians, adorable and full of mischief as kittens, become beautiful, loving companions when full grown.

Copper-eyed white female, Double Gr. and Qd. Ch. Windibank Patti-Kake of Azulita; Sire: Ch. Dixiland Dilli of Windibank; Dam: Ch. June Rose Bear of Dunesk; Breeder: Mrs. F.L. Tebbetts; Owner: Mrs. Walker K. Johnston.

You'll hate to part with any of the kittens, but a houseful of mischievous animals will probably be too much for you. You should have no trouble finding good homes for the litter. Your pet shop owner may be interested in buying a kitten. Word of mouth is usually the best advertisement, and friends who know that your Persian has had kittens will tell others. Don't be surprised if you find strangers on your doorsteps, eager for a kitten of their own. A notice placed on the bulletin board of your neighborhood market may also be used to good advantage in selling kittens, and an ad in your local newspaper is a tried and true method.

Cream male, Gr. and Double Ch. Longhill Michael II of Castila; Sire: Gr. Longhill's Michael; Dam: Longhill's Mazda; Breeder: Anthony De Santis; Owner: Mrs. Marcena Myers.

This proud owner has just finished grooming her Persian, and will anxiously await the judge's appraisal.

6. Showing Your Cat

A Persian cat's formal, or registered, name tells a good deal about him. The prefix such as "Dearheart" is the cattery name of the owner of the mother cat, or breeder. His given name comes next and, if the cat is later owned by another cattery, that name is added. A total of 25 letters is about the average permitted by most associations, which includes the prefix, or breeder's cattery, the given name of the cat, and the suffix, or owner's cattery. Thus, Dearheart Terry of Donegai was bred at Dearheart, but now belongs to Donegai Cattery.

There are five national organizations for the purpose of registering the names and pedigrees of purebred cats, longhairs, and shorthairs. These organizations also sanction shows and keep records of the wins made at the cat shows, which are put on by their affiliated clubs. The rules and procedures of each national organization differ slightly, but are very similar in all important respects. A cat may attain championship and grand championship status in any one association, or in all five associations. This accounts for the double, triple, etc., champion title preceding a show cat's name.

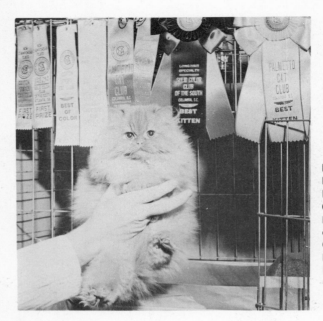

Red female, Ben-Mar Sparkle; Sire: Kohnioor Tim O'Cream; Dam: Moonfleet Tama of Ben-Mar; Owned and bred by Mr. & Mrs. B.G. Ehrhardt.

Red tabby peke face male, Gr. Ch. Rustnik Johnnie; Sire: Ch. Elco Rudolpho; Dam: Tr. Ch. Far fin Madeline of Rustnik; Owned and bred by Lorraine A. Wiesemann.

Brown tabby female, Gr. Ch. Minqua's Gingersnap of Co-Mc; Sire: Ch. Sunnyland Calumet of Minqua; Dam: Ch. Sunnyland Nerissa of Longhill; Breeder: Mr. and Mrs. Thomas Martinke; Owner: Mrs. C.A. Coughlin.

Calico female, Ch. Jay-Kay's Jeanamea; Sire: Ch. Spero's Sir George Bimbo; Dam: Queens Patches of Jay-Kay; Owned and bred by Dorothy B. Anderson.

Display cages are furnished at the show, and you may bring whatever accessories that you feel will best compliment your exhibit.

Each show has from 125 to 200 individual exhibitors showing a total of 175 to 300 cats. The Cat Fanciers' Association is the most popular registering organization because it has printed studbook records since 1909.

To briefly summarize show procedure, your entry is solicited and returned by you to the entry clerk approximately one month prior to the date of the show. Entries are recorded and catalogued according to breed, color, sex and classes. In the nonchampionship classes are kittens (4 to 8 months of age), altered cats and household pets. Championship classes are novice, open, champion and grand champion. The novice class is only for those cats over 8 months of age and, in some associations, under 2 years, who have not yet won a first, or blue, ribbon. The open class includes all cats who have not won the required number of points to claim their championships. Champion and grand champion classes, respectively, are for those who have achieved that status. Winners of the novice and open class of each sex compete for "winner's points," or points towards

Your cat is given an identifying number and entered in the official catalogue when you submit his name to be an entry in a show.

Tortoiseshell female, Qd. Ch. Shawnee Masquerade; Sire: Ch. Glad-Lows Red Coad; Dam: Shawnee Apache Topaz; Owned and bred by Mrs. Nikki Horner.

Copper-eyed white male, Qd. Gr. Ch. Shawnee's Moon-flight; Sire: Gr. Ch. Klinkhammer's Topper of Castilia; Dam: Gr. Ch. Shawnee Moon-flower; Owned and bred by Mrs. Nikki Horner.

Sealpoint Himalayan male, Hm. Tr. Ch. Chatelaine Al Hakim of Chestermere; Sire: Briarry Alcazar; Dam: Briarry Jett; Breeder: Mrs. G.M. Kirby Smith, England; Owner: Ben and Ann Borrett.

Copper-eyed white male, Rm. Double Gr. Ch. Klinkhammer's Charmer; Owner: Mrs. Kris Klinkhammer.

Red tabby male, Tr. Ch. Elco's Major Markwell; Sire: Ch. Elco's Fire Chief; Dam: Elco's Torti; Owned and bred by Ella Conroy.

Brown tabby male, Ch. Glen-Lyn Buster Brown; Sire: Qd. Ch. Glen-Lyn Don Tomas; Dam: Double Ch. Silver Vista Peachy Miss of Glen Lyn; Owned and bred by Mrs. James Elliott.

championship, in each breed and color. Those receiving these points then compete against the champion and grand champion first-place winners for best male, or female, of their color. Best of color and best of color opposite sex are picked from these two. Divisional bests are chosen from these best of colors and opposites. Then, in all-breed shows, best and opposite longhair, best and opposite shorthair, and finally best, second best, best opposite sex, and second best opposite sex in show. There are also wins given for best and best opposite sex of each class—novice, open, championship, etc., as well as for each of the nonchampionship groups. Usually a longhair and a shorthair specialty show is benched in conjunction with an all-breed show, with their own separate judges choosing their "bests" in each of the above categories also.

When you arrive at the show as an exhibitor, you are assigned to a display cage provided by the show management. You "furnish" the interior to your own taste in the way of draperies, etc., which will best show off your exhibit. Litter and food are usually provided for you to use. Your cat is listed and numbered in the official catalogue, but is judged by the number only. Judging cages are in a separate enclosure and are unmarked. The cat's number is placed on top of the judging cage and indicates the order in which he is to be brought to the judging area. He is placed in the cage from the rear, and the judge removes him from the front. Shows are open to the general public, and admission is charged. Further information about clubs and your local shows can be obtained by writing to the secretaries of the various national organizations. Your nearby club also can give you the names of breeders in your area.

Shaded silver male, Quint. Ch. Beverly-Serrano Roger of Dearheart; Sire: Tr. Ch. Sir Anthony Dearheart; Dam: Beverly-Serrano Mar-E; Breeder: V.O. Peterson; Owner: Dr. & Mrs. P.N. Ramsdale.

Mrs. Ramsdale, the author, gives one of her proud possessions an affectionate hug.

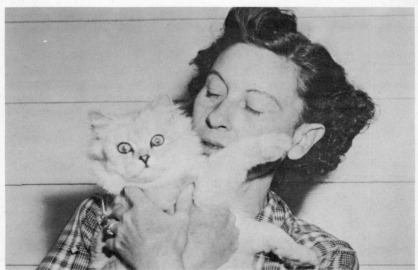

Red female, right, Qd. Ch. Kitturah's Kute Rusteena; Red male, left, Ch. Kitturah's Favorite Boy; both of same parents; Sire: Ch. Shawnee's Copper Top; Dam: Ch. Kitturah's Fletta; Owned and bred by Mrs. Robert E. Musser.

Blue smoke female, Double Ch. Silver Dawn's Denise; Sire:Worsley's Magnificent Teddy; Dam: Silver Dawn's Pumpkin; Owned and bred by Mrs. Max Eckenburg.

61

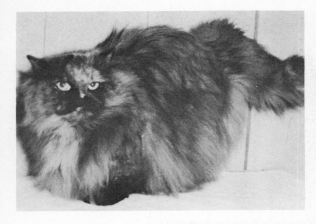

Tortoiseshell female, Ch. Shawnee Haloween; Sire: Double Ch. Shawnee Cooper Coach II; Dam: Ch. Longhills Mabel of Shawnee; Owned and bred by Mrs. Nikki Horner.

Blue male, Double Gr. Ch. Dixi-Land Queen of Azulita; Sire: Ch. Windibank Dear David of Dunesk (Imp.); Dam: Dixi-Land's Iana; Breeder: Mrs. J.H. Revington; Owner: Mrs. Walker K. Johnston.

Blue male, Ch. Vi-Jon's Gorgeous George; Sire: Gaymor Blue Robin; Dam: Bloemhill Fluffy; Owned and bred by Mrs. John Small.

White blue-eyed female, Double Ch. Galahad's Faith; Owned by Blanche Wolfram Smith.

Blue-eyed white female, Gr. Ch. Francine's Little Princess; Sire: Triple Ch. Akanta's Pierrot of Francines; Dam: Qd. Ch. Puckett's Kim My Girl; Owned and bred by Mrs. Stuart L. Puckett.

Chinchilla male, Triple G. Ch. Shy's Castle Jeffrey; Sire: Ch. Shy's Castle Perry; Dam: Ch. Shy Castle Lanette; Owned and bred by Mrs. Willard Shy.

Black male, Double Ch. Ayme-Tu-Wynn Rex of Larks-Purr; Sire: Gr. Ch. Great Lakes Le Duke of Rosemont; Dam: Tr. Ch. Ayme-Tu-Wynn Lady Alice; Breeder: Mrs. M.E. Thorne; Owner: Mrs. Jean F. Burrill.

Odd-eyed white male, Qn. Ch. Gallahad's Azhar of Shah-An-Shah; Sire: Ch. Evergreen White Pine of Akanta; Dam: Ch. Milky Way's Iris of Gallahad; Breeder: Blanche Wolfram; Owner: Mrs. Suzanne Barberio.